P9-CML-114

10/18

Explore Outer Space

SUPERNOVAS

by Ruth Owen

WINDMILL
BOOKS

New York

Published in 2013 by Windmill Books, An Imprint of Rosen Publishing
29 East 21st Street, New York, NY 10010

Produced for Windmill by Ruby Tuesday Books Ltd
Editor for Ruby Tuesday Books Ltd: Mark J. Sachner
US Editor: Sara Antill
Designer: Emma Randall
Consultant: Kevin Yates, Fellow of the Royal Astronomical Society

Photo Credits:
Cover © Superstock; 4–5, 8, 10–11, 24, 28–29 © Shutterstock; 6 © NASA, ESA, and J. Hester (ASU); 7 © NASA, ESA, STScl, J. Hester and P. Scowen (Arizona State University); 9 © NASA/ESA; 12–13 © NASA and The Hubble Heritage Team (STScl/AURA); 14–15 © NASA/CXC/Penn State/G. Garmire et al; 16–17 © NASA, ESA, J. Hester and A. Loll (Arizona State University); 18–19 © Science Photo Library; 20–21 © NASA/JPL–Caltech/UCLA; 22 (bottom) © Wikipedia (public domain); 22–23 © NASA/ESA/JHU/R.Sankrit & W.Blair; 25 (top) © ESO, P. Kervella, Digitized Sky Survey 2 and A. Fujii; 25 (bottom) © European Southern Observatory (ESO); 27 © Nathan Smith (University of California, Berkeley), and NASA.

Library of Congress Cataloging-in-Publication Data

Owen, Ruth, 1967–
 Supernovas / by Ruth Owen.
     p. cm. — (Explore outer space)
 Includes index.
 ISBN 978-1-4488-8078-2 (library binding) — ISBN 978-1-4488-8119-2 (pbk.) —
 ISBN 978-1-4488-8125-3 (6-pack)
 1. Supernovae—Juvenile literature. I. Title.
 QB843.S95O94 2013
 523.8'4465—dc23
                                   2012001527

Manufactured in the United States of America

CPSIA Compliance Information: Batch # B3S12WM: For Further Information contact Windmill Books, New York, New York at 1-866-478-0556

CONTENTS

A Bright Light in the Sky

On July 4, 1054, a bright light suddenly appeared in the sky. **Astronomers** in China witnessed the event and recorded the date. The Chacoan people of New Mexico also saw the light. They recorded its position in the night sky in a rock painting.

The Chacoan rock painting shows a star, a handprint, and a moon. Every 18.5 years the moon returns to the same position that the moon occupied around July 4, 1054. If you stand next to the rock painting and look through a telescope to the left of the moon, something wonderful can be seen. It's not the bright light the Chacoans saw, however.

The bright light in the sky, in 1054, was a **supernova**. A massive star had come to the end of its life and exploded. Today, where the Chacoans saw the death of a star, we can see a **nebula**, a vast cloud of gas and dust made up from the remains of that star.

That's Out of This World!

The 1054 supernova was visible in the night sky for about two years. For the first three weeks, it could even be seen in the daytime!

The Chacoan rock painting of the 1054 supernova can be seen at Chaco Canyon, in New Mexico. It is on the underside of a rocky overhang. In this photo, you are looking up at the painting.

THE LIVES OF STARS

Stars are massive balls of incredibly hot, burning gas. They give off light, heat, and **radiation**. Our star, the Sun, has been burning for about 4.5 billion years. Like all stars, the Sun was born, it will grow old, and finally, it will die.

Stars are born inside the clouds of gas and dust known as nebulae. Inside the cloud, the gas and dust break up into clumps. Under the weight of its own **gravity**, a clump will collapse in on itself. The pressure of gravity forces the gas and dust into a sphere, or ball.

Pressure builds as the material in the sphere is pressed together by gravity, and it gets hotter and hotter inside the sphere. When the temperature in the core reaches around 18 million degrees Fahrenheit (10 million degrees Celsius) the sphere ignites and begins to burn the gases it formed out of. A star is born!

This swirling, colorful cloud is part of the "star factory" named the Omega Nebula.

It might look like a rocky mountain, but this is part of the Eagle Nebula. Stars are forming in these fingerlike clumps of cloud.

That's Out of This World!

The nebulae in which stars form are often called "star nurseries" or "star factories." The gases and dust inside these nebulae are the ingredients for making stars.

THE DEATHS OF STARS

Our Sun is a medium-size star. Stars of this size slowly burn up their fuel and may live for billions of years. Eventually, however, their fuel supply runs out, and their lives come to an end.

As the star's fuel runs out, it swells in size and becomes a **red giant** star. Then the star begins to expel, or blow off, its outer layers. These layers of gas and dust form a cloud, known as a planetary nebula.

Finally, after a slow death lasting millions of years, the remains of the star's core collapse, leaving just a small, dense star called a **white dwarf**.

Massive stars, many times larger than our Sun, do not die slow deaths over millions of years. These stars end their lives in a more dramatic way.

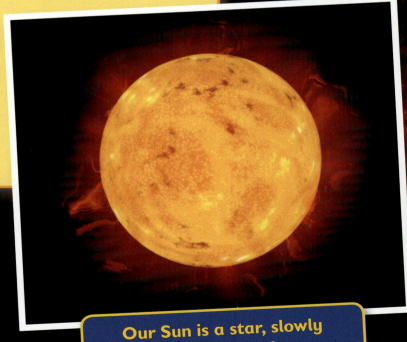

Our Sun is a star, slowly burning its store of gases.

The Helix Nebula is a planetary nebula. These nebulae get their name because they are sphere-shaped, like planets.

Gases and dust

That's Out of This World!

The remains of a star that have been squeezed by gravity to form a white dwarf are super compressed. In fact, a teaspoon of material from a white dwarf could weigh up to 100 tons (91 t). That's the same as about 50 cars!

SUPERNOVA!

Giant stars with over eight times the mass of the Sun burn up their fuel fast. These stars may live for just half a billion years.

As a giant star burns fuel, the process creates outward pressure. This is balanced by gravity, which creates inward pressure on the star. As the star's burning process slows down, however, the outward pressure drops.

When this happens, the star swells to become a **red supergiant**. Inside, however, its core is shrinking, crushed by the inward pressure of gravity. Forces inside the star keep it burning, but eventually all its fuel is gone.

In a microsecond, the inward pressure on the star's core crushes it to such an extent that it reaches temperatures of billions of degrees Fahrenheit (Celsius). The core cannot take any more. It collapses, causing a giant shockwave that blows the star apart in a supernova—an explosion so big and so hot that it's impossible to imagine!

That's Out of This World!

As a giant star's core is crushed and collapses in the final few seconds of its life, it shrinks from thousands of miles (km) in diameter to just 10 to 12 miles (16–19 km)!

Artwork showing a supernova

SUPERNOVA STARDUST

When a giant star explodes in a supernova, a huge cloud of matter is blasted into space. The cloud may look like nothing more than gas and dust, but it contains the essential ingredients for making new stars, new planets—in fact, everything we know of!

As a massive star burns out, **elements** such as oxygen, carbon, and iron are created in its core. Other elements, such as sodium, chlorine, potassium, calcium, and gold are created in the intense heat of its eventual supernova explosion. These elements form part of the giant cloud, or nebula, created by the explosion.

This supernova stardust travels out into space at speeds of up to 25,000 miles per second (40,000 km/s). As the cloud expands, it gathers up more space gas and dust, like a giant snowplow gathering up snow before it.

The nebula, sometimes called a **supernova remnant,** will continue to expand outward and outward. In time, material in the cloud will be recycled and become new stars and planets.

Cassiopeia A

That's Out of This World!

Cassiopeia A is a vast cloud of matter left over from a supernova that happened in our **galaxy**, the **Milky Way**, about 340 years ago. The material is still moving away from the point of the explosion at speeds of about 31 million miles per hour (50 million km/h).

Neutron Stars and Black Holes

At first, the supernova shines brighter than all the other stars in its galaxy. Then, its light quickly fades. Where once there was a giant star, all that is left is a tiny, dense, fast-spinning **neutron star**.

During its death, the star's core was crushed so much that the remaining neutron star may measure just 12 miles (19 km) in diameter. However, it will contain 1.4 times as much matter as our Sun, which measures 865,000 miles (1.4 million km) in diameter!

Some giant stars are so massive—about 10 times the size of our Sun—that they leave behind a larger core. This larger core collapses under its own gravity. It becomes an incredibly compact, dense object called a **black hole**. The gravity of a black hole is so powerful that nothing in its **orbit** can escape being pulled into it.

RCW 103 is the cloud of remains from a supernova that happened about 2,000 years ago.

This blue light is the neutron star that was left behind after the supernova.

That's Out of This World!

A neutron star is so dense that, on Earth, a piece the size of a sugar cube would weigh as much as Mount Everest.

THE CRAB NEBULA

The bright light in the sky witnessed and recorded by the Chacoan people was the death of a giant star with 10 times the mass of our Sun!

Today, we are left with evidence of the 1054 supernova event in the form of a vast cloud of supernova remnants, called the Crab Nebula.

So when we say the Crab Nebula is vast, just how large is that? The Crab Nebula has a diameter of about 64,000,000,000,000 miles (103 trillion km)! Another way to present this measurementis in **light years**.

The fastest thing we know of is light. It travels at about 186,500 miles per second (300,000 km/s). A light year is the distance light travels in one year. Astronomers use light years as a unit of measurement to measure great distances in space.

In light years, the Crab Nebula's diameter is about 11 light years. It's still the same huge distance, but far fewer zeros to handle!

That's Out of This World!

The cloud of gas and dust caused by the 1054 supernova is still expanding. Material is moving away from the site of the explosion at 930 miles per second (1,500 km/s).

The Crab Nebula

The bluish glow inside the Crab Nebula is caused by the light of a neutron star— all that remains of the once-giant star.

MORE SUPERNOVAS

Sometimes a supernova occurs when two stars "live" close together in what is called a **binary star system.**

When one of the stars dies and becomes a white dwarf, it gets smaller and denser. The very dense white dwarf has a strong gravitational pull, though. It begins to pull material from its companion star.

As the white dwarf's mass increases, this puts greater inward pressure on its core. Finally, the pressure gets too great, and the white dwarf explodes in a supernova.

These types of supernovas are brighter than those caused by the deaths of giant stars. Each one of these supernovas gives off the same amount of brightness, too. So, if one white dwarf supernova looks dimmer than another, it doesn't mean it was just a smaller explosion. It means it is farther from Earth. Using the different brightness levels of these supernovas helps astronomers measure distances in space.

The companion star

Artwork showing a binary star system

A white dwarf star

Material gathered by the white dwarf from its companion star

The First Recorded Supernova

Throughout human history, people must have looked to the skies and seen bright lights appear and then disappear.

The first actual record of a supernova being witnessed and then documented, however, was in AD 185. Chinese astronomers saw a new star appear in the sky, then disappear eight months later. They called it a "guest star" and recorded its appearance and disappearance in *The Book of the Later Han*. This book told the history of China from AD 25 to AD 220.

The ancient astronomers' records gave modern-day astronomers the date of the supernova and its approximate location in space. In 2006, scientists were able to calculate that a supernova remnant named RCW 86 is the remains of the supernova that happened in AD 185.

The AD 185 supernova has been named SN 185. It's an example of a supernova caused by an exploding white dwarf star.

That's Out of This World!

The bright light of supernova SN 185 could be seen in the sky for eight months. Its cloud of remains, RCW 86, is 8,500 light years from Earth.

These red clouds of dust are the supernova remnant RCW 86.

KEPLER'S STAR

With the Milky Way home to billions of stars, astronomers estimate that we should witness a supernova in our home galaxy at least every 100 years. Unfortunately for astronomers, no supernova has been seen in the Milky Way for over 400 years!

The last time a supernova was seen in our galaxy was 1604. This supernova is often called "Kepler's Star," after German astronomer Johannes Kepler, who witnessed and recorded the event.

At the time, telescopes had not been invented. The supernova was so bright, however, that it was visible with the naked eye, even though it happened 20,000 light years from Earth. The "new star" could even be seen during the day for over three weeks!

Astronomers think that other supernovas might have happened in the Milky Way since 1604. They may, however, have been hidden from view by dust clouds.

Johannes Kepler

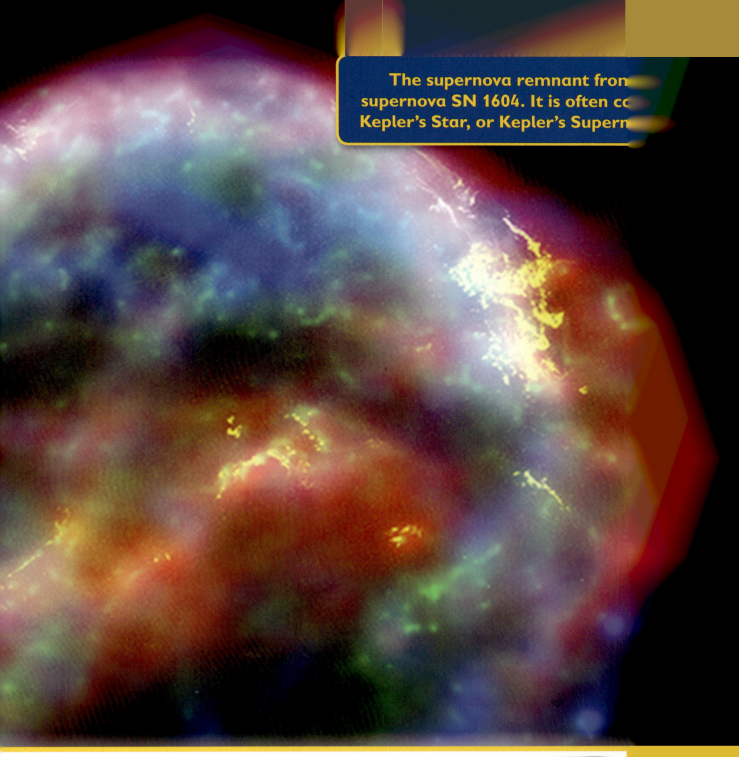

The supernova remnant from supernova SN 1604. It is often c Kepler's Star, or Kepler's Supern

That's Out of This World!

It can be mind-boggling to think of, but it's important to remember that if an event, such as the 1604 supernova, happens 20,000 light years from Earth, that means it happened 20,000 years before it could be seen on Earth. When Johannes Kepler saw the light from the 1604 supernova, that light had been traveling through space toward Earth for 20,000 years!

If a supernova should occur in our galaxy at least every 100 years, are there any stars that are looking like good candidates to become our next Milky Way supernova? The answer to that question is, yes!

Betelgeuse is a giant star, just 500 light years from Earth. It has a mass 20 times that of our Sun and is the eighth brightest star in our night sky. Unlike our Sun, which is 4.5 billion years old and is only halfway through its life, Betelgeuse is just 10 million years old, but it is already beginning to die.

Astronomers believe that Betelgeuse could explode in a supernova very soon. In space terms, very soon could mean in one million years. However, it could also mean within your lifetime!

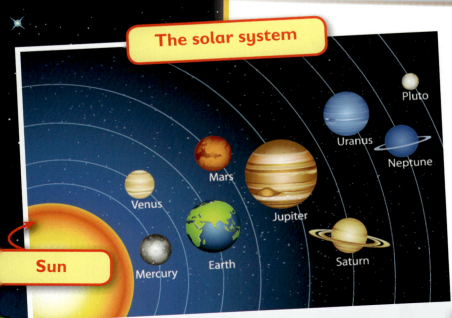

The solar system

Sun

Pluto

Uranus

Neptune

Mars

Venus

Jupiter

Mercury

Earth

Saturn

That's Out of This World!

Betelgeuse is
that if it repl
Sun at the cen
solar system,
extend beyon
Venus, Earth,
In fact, it's
it would sw
everything as
as Jupi

Images of Betelgeuse from the European Southern Observatory's Very Large Telescope

One of the four telescopes at the European Southern Observatory's Very Large Telescope, in Chile

MOST LIKELY TO EXPLODE

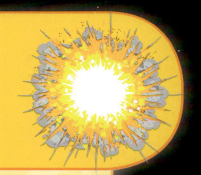

Around 8,000 light years from Earth is one of the most visible and massive stars in our galaxy—Eta Carinae.

In 1843, Eta Carinae suffered an explosion, blasting material out into space. At first, astronomers thought the star had been destroyed in a supernova. Eta Carinae survived, however, and is now buried inside two clouds of gas and dust.

Eta Carinae is burning up fast, though, and astronomers believe it will supernova in the next few thousand years. It could, however, explode much sooner.

In 2004, in a galaxy 70 million light years from the Milky Way, a star experienced an explosion similar to the 1843 Eta Carinae blast. Just like Eta Carinae, this distant star survived the blast. Just two years later, however, it exploded in a full-blown supernova. If Eta Carinae follows a similar pattern to this distant star, that means it could supernova at any time!

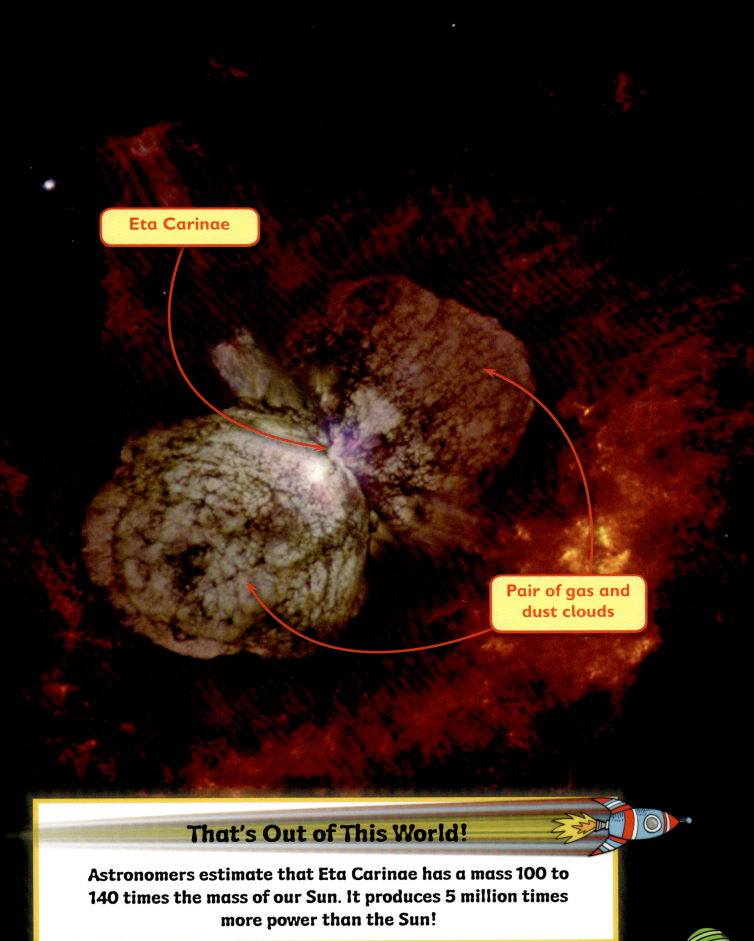

Eta Carinae

Pair of gas and dust clouds

That's Out of This World!

Astronomers estimate that Eta Carinae has a mass 100 to 140 times the mass of our Sun. It produces 5 million times more power than the Sun!

KEEP WATCHING THE SKIES!

In September 2011, astronomers got the chance to view and study a supernova. The supernova, named PTF11kly, happened in the Pinwheel Galaxy, 21 million light years from Earth.

The supernova was from the explosion of a white dwarf star. Astronomers will be able to use the brightness of the supernova to take measurements of the universe. This is important because our universe is expanding, or growing outward. Measuring distances in the universe allows astronomers to keep records of how fast the universe is expanding outward.

No one knows when we will next see a supernova. Perhaps one has already happened in our Milky Way galaxy. Betelgeuse is 500 light years from Earth, so when it explodes in a supernova, it will take 500 years for the light of the explosion to reach us. Maybe a view of an amazing supernova is heading our way right now!

Stars in the Milky Way galaxy

That's Out of This World!

Before a star explodes, its collapsing core releases tiny particles called neutrinos. Neutrinos can be detected here on Earth before the supernova appears. SNEWS (SuperNova Early Warning System) is a network of neutrino detectors that gives astronomers advance notice that a supernova has occurred.

GLOSSARY

astronomers (uh-STRAH-nuh-merz) Scientists who specialize in the study of outer space.

binary star system (BY-nuh-ree STAHR SIS-tem) Two stars orbiting around one another. The brighter star is called the primary star, and the other star is its companion star.

black hole (BLAK HOHL) A region of space around a very small and extremely massive object, usually formed by a collapsed star, within which the gravitational field is so strong that not even light can escape.

elements (EH-luh-ments) Pure chemical substances that are found in nature. Hydrogen and helium are the most abundant elements in the universe, and iron is the most abundant element making up planet Earth.

galaxy (GA-lik-see) A group of stars, dust, gas, and other objects held together in outer space by gravity.

gravity (GRA-vih-tee) The force that causes objects to be attracted toward Earth's center or toward other physical bodies in space, such as stars or planets.

light year (LYT YIR) The distance light can travel in a year—more than 5.8 trillion miles (9.4 trillion km).

mass (MAS) The quantity of matter in a physical body that causes it to have weight when acted upon by gravity.

Milky Way (MIL-kee WAY) The galaxy that includes Earth and the rest of our Sun's solar system.

nebula (NEH-byuh-luh) (*plural nebulae*) A massive cloud of dust and gas in outer space. Many nebulae are formed by the collapse of stars, releasing matter that may, over millions or billions of years, clump together to form new stars.

neutron star (NOO-tron STAHR) A very compact, dense star that has collapsed under its own gravity.

rbit (OR-bit) To circle in a curved
ath around another object.

adiation (ray-dee-AY-shun) Energy
hat is given off, or radiated, in
ays, waves, or particles. The Sun
nay radiate energy in the form of
isible light waves (sunlight), harmful
ltraviolet waves, or microwaves.

ed giant (RED JY-ant) A star that
nearing the end of its life cycle.
s it uses up its energy, it grows in
ze and the temperature of its outer
tmosphere begins to cool off, giving
a reddish-orange color.

ed supergiant
RED SOO-per-jy-int) A star that is
ur larger in terms of size and volume
nan any others in the universe as it
ears the end of its life cycle. A red
upergiant may have a radius from

the center outward extending more
than seven times the distance of
Earth from our Sun.

supernova (soo-per-NOH-vuh)
A super-bright explosion of a star
that creates a sudden release of
energy and light. Its remains may
form nebulae.

supernova remnant
(soo-per-NOH-vuh REHM-nint)
The cloud of materials left behind
by the gigantic explosion of a star
in a supernova.

white dwarf (WYT DWARF)
A small, very dense star at the end
of its life cycle that has thrown off
most of its outer material, creating
a planetary nebula around it and
leaving only the hot core of the star
burning brightly at the center.

WEBSITES

**For web resources related to the subject of this book,
go to: www.windmillbooks.com/weblinks
and select this book's title.**

READ MORE

Croswell, Ken. *The Lives of Stars*. Honesdale, PA: Boyds Mills Press, 2009.

Galat, Joan Marie. *Black Holes and Supernovas*. Fact Finders: The Solar System and Beyond. Mankato, MN: Capstone Press, 2011.

Goldmsith, Mike. *Amazing Space Q & A*. New York: DK Publishing, 2011.

INDEX